The Pizza Cookbook

25 Delicious Pizza Recipes

By

Martha Stone

License Notes

No part of this Book can be reproduced in any form or by any means including print, electronic, scanning or photocopying unless prior permission is granted by the author.

All ideas, suggestions and guidelines mentioned here are written for informative purposes. While the author has taken every possible step to ensure accuracy, all readers are advised to follow information at their own risk. The author cannot be held responsible for personal and/or commercial damages in case of misinterpreting and misunderstanding any part of this Book.

About the author

Martha Stone is a chef and also cookbook writer. She was born and raised in Idaho where she spent most of her life growing up. Growing up in the country taught her how to appreciate and also use fresh ingredients in her cooking. This love for using the freshest ingredients turned into a passion for cooking. Martha loves to teach others how to cook and she loves every aspect of cooking from preparing the dish to smelling it cooking and sharing it with friends.

Martha eventually moved to California and met the love of her life. She settled down and has two children. She is a stay at home mom and involves her children in her cooking as much as possible. Martha decided to start writing cookbooks so that she could share her love for food and cooking with everyone else.

For a complete list of my published books, please, visit my Author's Page...

http://www.amazon.com/Martha-Stone/e/B00FDU8GR6/

You can also check out my blog at: http://martha-stone.blogspot.com or my Facebook at: https://www.facebook.com/marthastone2013

Table of Contents

Introduction

Pizza is a flat bread baked in oven and normally topped with cheese and tomato sauce. It is generally added with a choice of vegetables, meats and condiments. The contemporary pizza was originally invented in Italy and now the pizza and its variants have become very popular throughout the world.

Cooking

Pizza can be prepared in stone brick oven or in electric oven. One more option is a grilled pizza, for which its crust is baked on barbeque grill directly. Greek-style pizza is baked in pan rather than baked directly on bricks of oven.

Crust

The base of the pizza is called as the "crust". It may vary according to the style – thick like in Chicago-style or thin like in New York-style etc. Traditionally it is plain, but can also be stuffed with any kind of cheese or seasoned with herbs or garlic.

Cheese

Originally only mozzarella cheese was being used for pizzas. Nowadays, other varieties of cheeses such as Ricotta, Pecorino Romano, provolone etc, are also being used for pizzas.

Toppings

There are innumerable toppings that are used over pizzas. Those include, but are not limited to-

Artichoke, Bell pepper, Bacon, Carrot, Corn, Chili pepper, Feta, Ground beef, Garlic, Ham, Mushroom, Jalapeño, Onion, Olives, Pepperoni, Sausage, Spinach, Seafood, Sun-dried tomato, Tomato, etc.

Let us explore into the world of delicious pizza recipes!

1) Quick English-Muffin Pizza

"This is a quick and kid-friendly kind of pizza! Cheese, Pizza sauce, and topping make this a great meal of anytime or snack!"

Prep Time: 10 minutes

Cooking Time: 10 minutes

Ready In: 20 minutes

Yields: 4 servings

Ingredients:

- 4 English-muffins, split
- ½ cup of canned pizza-sauce
- 16 slices of pepperoni sausage
- 2 cups of mozzarella cheese, shredded

Directions:

1) Preheat oven at 375 degrees F (190 degrees C).

2) Lay English-muffin halves with cut-side up on a baking tray. Spread some pizza sauce on each muffin half. Top them with pepperoni slices and mozzarella cheese.

3) Bake them in oven for about 10 minutes, or till the cheese melts and becomes browned on edges.

2) Time-Pass Pizza

"This is a favourite pizza of Kids and Adults too! We can add any vegetable we want."

Prep Time: 5 minutes

Cooking Time: 5 minutes

Ready In: 10 minutes

Yields: 2 servings

Ingredients:

- 2 matzo crackers
- ¼ cup of spaghetti sauce
- 1 dash of dry oregano
- ¼ cup of black olives, sliced
- ¾ cup of mozzarella cheese, shredded
- 1 dash of garlic salt
- 1 tomato, thinly sliced

Directions:

1) Preheat the oven at 350 F (175 C).

2) Spread matzo pieces with spaghetti sauce. Sprinkle oregano and garlic salt on sauce. Cover it with mozzarella cheese, olive slices, and slices of tomato. Place the pizzas on baking sheet.

3) Bake them in oven, for about 5 minutes, or till cheese is melted.

3) Pepperoni Baked Pizza

"This pan-pizza can be prepared very quickly!"

Prep Time: 10 minutes

Cooking Time: 20 minutes

Ready In: 40 minutes

Yields: 6 servings

Ingredients:

- 1 (16.3 oz.) can of Pillsbury Home-style refrigerated biscuits
- 16 slices of pepperoni
- 1 (8 oz.) can of pizza sauce
- 2 slices of mozzarella cheese, shredded

Directions:

1) Cut all biscuits into 8 pieces each; toss them with1 cup of cheese and pizza sauce.

2) Lay them in a greased baking dish. Top them with remaining 1 cup of cheese and pepperoni.

3) Bake them in oven for about 20 minutes or till bubbly and golden brown.

4) White Pizza

"It is very easy to prepare but really pretty yummy!"

Prep Time: 10 minutes

Cooking Time: 15 minutes

Ready In: 25 minutes

Yields: 1 12-inch pizza

Ingredients:

- 2 tbsp. of extra-virgin olive-oil, divided
- 8 cloves of garlic, quartered
- 1 (12-inch) thin pizza-crust, pre-baked
- 3 cups of mozzarella cheese, shredded

Directions:

1) Preheat oven at 450 F (230 degrees C).

2) Place pre-baked pizza crust on the baking tray; drizzle it with 1 tbsp. of olive-oil. Sprinkle mozzarella cheese over pizza crust evenly; top it with garlic pieces.

3) Bake it in oven till cheese begins to brown and becomes bubbly, for about 15 minutes. Drizzle it with some more olive-oil; cut it into small wedges and serve.

5) Gorgonzola Cheesy Pizza with Pear

"This is an appetizer pizza with the unique combination of typical Gorgonzola and fragrant pears."

Prep Time: 10 minutes

Cooking Time: 15 minutes

Ready In: 25 minutes

Yields: 1 pizza

Ingredients:

- 1 (16 oz.) pkg. of pizza-crust dough, refrigerated
- 4 oz. of provolone cheese, sliced
- 2 oz. of walnuts, chopped
- 2 ½ oz. Gorgonzola cheese, crumbled
- 1 Bosc pear, sliced thinly
- 2 tbsp. of fresh chives, chopped

Directions:

1) Preheat the oven at 450 F (230 C).

2) Place pizza-crust dough over a baking tray. Lay slices of Provolone cheese over the pizza. Top the cheese using slices of pear. On the top, sprinkle with Gorgonzola cheese and walnuts.

3) Bake it in oven for 8 to 10 minutes, or till cheese melts and crust becomes lightly browned. Remove it from oven. Top the pizza with fresh chives. Cut into wedges and serve.

6) Buffalo-Wing Style Chicken Pizza

"This is pizza with a punch of buffalo-wing flavour!"

Prep Time: 30 minutes

Cooking Time: 25 minutes

Ready In: 55 minutes

Yields: 6 servings

Ingredients:

- 3 boneless and skinless chicken-breast halves, cooked
- 2 tbsp. of butter, melted
- 1 (8 oz.) bottle of blue-cheese salad-dressing
- 1 (16-inch) pizza crust, prebaked
- 1 (2 oz.) bottle of hot sauce
- 1 (8 oz.) pkg. of mozzarella cheese, shredded

Directions:

1) Preheat the oven at 425 F (220 C).

2) Cut the cooked chicken into cubes. Combine cubed chicken, hot sauce and melted butter in a bowl and mix well. Spread Cheese salad-dressing over the crust and top it with the chicken mixture; sprinkle it with mozzarella cheese.

3) Bake in it oven till cheese becomes bubbly and crust becomes golden brown, for about 5-10 minutes. Allow it to set for a few minutes prior to cutting into slices and serve.

7) Pinwheel Pizzas

"This is a great recipe for kids. It is greatly suitable for parties as well!"

Prep Time: 20 minutes

Cooking Time: 12 minutes

Ready In: 32 minutes

Yields: 16 pinwheel pizzas

Ingredients:

- 1 (8 oz.) can of crescent -roll dough, refrigerated
- 2 cups of mozzarella cheese, shredded
- 1 (14 oz.) can of pizza sauce
- 24 slices of pepperoni

Directions:

1) Preheat the oven at 375 F (190 C).

2) Form 8 crescent-roll dough triangles into 4 rectangles on a baking tray. Place 6 pepperoni slices and equal amount of cheese over each rectangle. Roll them lengthwise tightly; slice each roll into 4-5 pieces.

3) Bake the roll pieces in oven till golden brown, for about 12 minutes. Serve the pinwheel pizzas along with pizza-sauce for dipping.

8) Vegetable Pizza

"We can use low-fat sour cream in this pizza recipe, if desired."

Prep Time: 25 minutes

Cooking Time: 10 minutes

Ready In: 2 hrs 25 minutes

Yields: 16 servings

Ingredients:

- 1 cup of sour cream
- 2 (8 oz) pkg. of crescent rolls, refrigerated
- 1 tsp of dry dill weed
- ¼ tsp of garlic salt
- 1 onion, chopped finely
- 1 stalk of celery, sliced thinly
- 1 red bell-pepper, chopped
- 1½ cups of broccoli, chopped
- 1 (8 oz) pkg. of cream-cheese, softened
- 1 (1 oz) pkg. of ranch dressing-mix
- ½ cup of radishes, halved and sliced thinly
- 1 carrot, grated

Directions:

1. Preheat the oven at 350 F (175 C). Coat one jelly-roll pan with cooking spray.

2. Fill jelly-roll pan with crescent-roll dough. Allow it to stand for 5 minutes. Prick it with a fork.

3. Bake it in oven for 10 minutes and allow it to cool.

4. Mix cream cheese, sour cream, garlic salt, dill weed and ranch dressing-mix in a mixing bowl. Spread this cream mixture over the top of crust. Arrange onion, celery, carrot, bell pepper, radish and broccoli on the top of cream mixture. Cover and allow it to chill. After chilled, cut the pizza into wedges and serve.

9) BBQ-Style Chicken Pizza

"The topping of this pizza with barbeque sauce, cilantro, diced chicken, peppers, and onion is very tasty!"

Prep Time: 30 minutes

Cooking Time: 15 minutes

Ready In: 45 minutes

Yields: 1 12-inch pizza

Ingredients:

- 1 (12-inch) pizza crust, pre-baked
- 1 cup of spicy barbeque-sauce
- ½ cup of fresh cilantro, chopped
- 1 cup of pepperoncini peppers, sliced
- 2 cups of Colby-Monterey Jack cheese, shredded
- 2 skinless and boneless chicken-breast halves, cooked and cut into cubes
- 1 cup of red onion, chopped

Directions:

1) Preheat the oven at 350 F (175 C).

2) Place the pizza crust over a baking tray. Spread barbeque sauce over the crust. Top it with cilantro, chicken, onion, pepperoncini peppers, and cheese.

3) Bake it in oven for about 15 minutes, or till cheese melts and becomes bubbly.

10) Mixed Cheesy Margarita Pizza

"This Italian classic pizza is really simple to prepare and incredibly delicious to taste!"

Prep Time: 15 minutes

Cooking Time: 10 minutes

Ready In: 40 minutes

Yields: 2 pizzas

Ingredients:

- ¼ cup of olive oil
- 1 tbsp. of garlic, minced
- 8 Roma tomatoes, sliced
- 2 (12 inch) pizza crusts, pre-baked
- 4 oz. of Fontina cheese, shredded
- ½ cup of feta cheese, crumbled
- 8 oz. of Mozzarella cheese, shredded
- ½ cup of Parmesan cheese, freshly grated
- 10 leaves of fresh basil, washed
- ½ tsp of sea salt

Directions:

1) Mix together garlic, olive oil, and salt in a bowl; add tomatoes and toss; allow it to stand for about 15 minutes. Preheat the oven at 400 F (200 C).

2) Spread some tomato marinade over each pizza crust. Evenly sprinkle pizza crusts with Fontina and Mozzarella cheeses. Layer tomatoes over the top and sprinkle with basil and shredded feta and Parmesan cheese.

3) Bake them in oven till cheese becomes golden brown and bubbly, for about 10 minutes.

11) BBQ Style Grilled Chicken Pizza

"This is a different version of traditional pizza using BBQ sauce!"

Prep Time: 20 minutes

Cooking Time: 10 minutes

Ready In: 30 minutes

Yields: 4 servings

Ingredients:

- 1 (12 inch) pizza crust, pre-baked
- ½ cup of barbecue sauce
- 1 cup of Monterey-Jack cheese, shredded
- ¼ cup of red bell-pepper, chopped
- ¼ cup of green bell-pepper, chopped
- ¼ cup of red onion, chopped
- ½ cup of grilled chicken, diced

Directions:

1) Preheat the oven at 450 F (230 C).

2) Place the pizza crust on a baking sheet. Spread barbecue sauce over the crust. Distribute diced chicken on top. Evenly sprinkle with onion, green pepper and red pepper. Cover it with cheese.

3) Bake the crust in oven for about 10-12 minutes, or till cheese melts.

12) Red-Sauce less Pizza

"This is a great alternative to the traditional red-sauce pizza for the people who don't like red-sauce but love pizzas!"

Prep Time: 15 minutes

Cooking Time: 20 minutes

Ready In: 35 minutes

Yields: 8 servings

Ingredients:

- 2 tbsp. of butter, melted
- 1 tbsp. of olive oil
- 2 tbsp. of sun-dried tomato pesto
- 1 tsp of dry basil leaves
- 1 tbsp. of Parmesan cheese, grated
- 1 pizza crust, unbaked
- 1 bunch of fresh spinach, torn
- 1 sweet onion, sliced
- 1 jalapeno pepper, chopped
- 3 tbsp. of garlic, minced
- 1 tsp of dry oregano
- 1 tomato, sliced
- 1 (6 oz.) pkg. of feta cheese, crumbled

Directions:

1) Preheat the oven as per pizza-crust package directions.

2) Mix olive oil, butter, pesto, garlic, basil, Parmesan cheese and oregano in a bowl. Evenly spread this mixture over pizza crust.

3) Layer tomato, onion, spinach, and jalapeno over the pizza. Top it with feta cheese.

4) Bake it as per pizza-crust package directions.

13) Pesto and Chicken Pizza

"This is a simple and easy pizza that can be used for a great meal. Fontina can be substituted with mozzarella."

Prep Time: 10 minutes

Cooking Time: 10 minutes

Ready In: 20 minutes

Yields: 6 servings

Ingredients:

- ½ cup of pesto-basil sauce
- 1 (12-inch) pizza crust, pre-baked
- 1 (6 oz.) jar of artichoke hearts, drained
- 2 cups of chicken-breast strips, cooked
- ½ cup of fontina cheese, shredded

Directions:

1) Preheat oven at 450 F (230 C).

2) Spread the pizza crust with pesto sauce. Layer artichoke hearts and chicken pieces over sauce. Sprinkle it with cheese.

3) Bake it in oven for about 8 to 10 minutes, till cheese melts and browned lightly at edges.

14) Slow Cooker Beef and Pasta Pizza

"This pizza with Ground beef and noodles is prepared in a slow cooker!"

Prep Time: 20 minutes

Cooking Time: 4 hrs

Ready In: 4 hrs 20 minutes

Servings: 6 servings

Ingredients:

- 1½ lb of ground beef
- 1 (8 oz.) pkg. of pepperoni sausage, sliced
- 1 (10.75 oz.) can of condensed-cream of tomato-soup
- 2 (14 oz.) jars of pizza sauce
- 1 (16 oz.) pkg. of mozzarella cheese, shredded
- 1 (8 oz.) pkg. of rigatoni pasta

Directions:

1. Boil a pot of slightly salted water. Add pasta to boiled water; cook for about 8 to 10 minutes or till al dente; drain the pasta and keep aside. In a medium skillet, brown beef on medium-high heat. Drain any excess grease.

2. In a slow cooker, arrange ground beef, cooked noodles, cheese, tomato soup, pizza sauce and pepperoni in alternate layers.

3. Cook them over Low-setting for about 4 hours.

15) Pizza with Hummus Spread

"This is a healthy and unique pizza which is prepared using hummus spread as an alternative of regular red sauce!"

Prep Time: 15 minutes

Cooking Time: 15 minutes

Ready In: 30 minutes

Yields: 8 servings

Ingredients:

- 1 (10 oz.) can of pizza-crust dough, refrigerated
- 1 cup of hummus spread
- 1 cup of broccoli florets
- 1½ cups of bell peppers (of any color), sliced
- 2 cups of Monterey-Jack cheese, shredded

Directions:

1) Preheat oven at 475 C (220 C).

2) Roll out the pizza-crust; place it on a baking sheet. Spread the crust with a layer of hummus spread. Arrange broccoli and pepper slices on hummus; top it with shredded Jack cheese.

3) Bake it in oven for about 10-15 minutes, till cheese melts in centre and crust becomes golden brown. Slice the pizza and serve.

16) Pesto and Veggie Pizza

"This pizza is a good alternative for regular kind of pizza!"

Prep Time: 10 minutes

Cooking Time: 10 minutes

Ready In: 20 minutes

Yields: 6 servings

Ingredients:

- 1 (12-inch) pizza crust, pre-baked
- ½ cup of pesto
- 1 cup of feta cheese, crumbled
- 1 (2 oz.) can of black olives, drained and chopped
- 1 (4 oz.) can of artichoke hearts, sliced and drained
- ½ cup of green bell-pepper, chopped
- 1 ripe tomato, chopped
- ½ small red-onion, chopped

Directions:

1. Preheat the oven at 450 F (230 C).

2. Spread the pizza crust with pesto. Top it with tomatoes, olives, bell peppers, artichoke hearts, red onions and cheese.

3. Bake it in oven for about 8 to 10 minutes, or till cheese melts and becomes browned.

17) Veggie and Mushroom Pizza

"This is another version of vegetable pizza which can be prepared very quickly and easily."

Prep Time: 10 minutes

Cooking Time: 12 minutes

Ready In: 22 minutes

Yields: 2 servings

Ingredients:

- 1 (12-inch) pizza crust, pre-baked
- 2 tbsp. of olive oil
- ½ cup of onion, sliced
- 1 cup of fresh mushrooms, sliced
- ¼ cup of black olives, chopped
- ½ cup of green bell-pepper, chopped
- 1 cup of tomato sauce, seasoned
- 2 cups of mozzarella cheese, shredded

Directions:

1) Preheat oven 350 F (175 C).

2) Place pizza crust over a baking tray. Evenly coat the crust with olive-oil. Spread the crust with tomato sauce. Evenly sprinkle vegetables over sauce and top it with shredded cheese.

3) Bake it in oven for about 10-12 minutes, or till cheese melts and becomes bubbly. Allow it cool for about 2-3 minutes prior to cutting. Cut it into wedges and serve.

18) Mushroom and Spinach Pizza

"This simple pizza with mushroom and spinach is better than regular pizza!"

Prep Time: 13 minutes

Cooking Time: 12 minutes

Ready In: 25 minutes

Yields: 1 12- inch pizza

Ingredients:

- 1 cup of fresh mushrooms, sliced
- 3 tbsp. of olive oil
- 1 tsp of sesame oil
- 1 cup of fresh spinach, cleaned and dried
- 8 oz. of mozzarella cheese, shredded
- 1 (12-inch) pizza crust, pre-baked

Directions:

1) Preheat the oven at 350 F (175 C). Place the pizza-crust on baking tray.

2) Mix sesame oil and olive oil together in a bowl. Coat pizza crust with this oil mixture, covering whole surface. Cut spinach leaves into ½-inch strips lengthwise and evenly spread them over the crust. Cover the pizza with mozzarella cheese; top it with mushrooms slices.

3) Bake it in oven for about 8-10 minutes, or till cheese melts and edges become brown and crisp.

19) Thai-Style Spicy Chicken Pizza

"This spicy chicken pizza is very easy to prepare and is inspired by Thai-style cooking"

Prep Time: 10 minutes

Cooking Time: 10 minutes

Ready In: 20 minutes

Yields: 8 servings

Ingredients:

- 1 (12-inch) pizza crust, pre-baked
- 1 (7 oz.) jar of peanut sauce
- 8 oz. of skinless and boneless chicken-breast halves, cooked and cut into strips
- 1 cup of Italian cheese-blend, shredded
- ¼ cup of peanut butter
- 1 bunch of green onions, chopped
- 1 tbsp. of roasted peanuts, chopped (optional)
- ½ cup of fresh bean-sprouts (optional)
- ½ cup of carrot, shredded (optional)

Directions:

1) Preheat oven at 400 F (200 C).

2) Combine peanut butter and peanut sauce in a bowl. Spread this mixture over pizza crust. Layer chicken strips on the top. Sprinkle it with cheese and green onions.

3) Bake it in oven for about 8-12 minutes, till cheese melts and become bubbly. Top it with carrot shreds, peanuts (if using), and bean-sprouts. Cut the pizza into slices and serve.

20) Chicken and Cranberry Brie Pizza

"This pizza can be prepared easily using an interesting blend of brie chicken, and cranberry."

Prep Time: 20 minutes

Cooking Time: 20 minutes

Ready In: 40 minutes

Yields: 4 servings

Ingredients:

- 2 chicken-breast halves, skinless and boneless
- 1 tbsp. of vegetable oil
- 1½ cups of cranberry sauce
- 6 oz. of Brie cheese, chopped
- 1 (12-inch) pizza crust, pre-baked
- 8 oz. of mozzarella cheese, shredded

Directions:

1) Preheat the oven at 350 F (175 C).

2) Cut the chicken-breasts into bite-sized pieces. In a skillet, heat oil till hot. Add chicken; sauté till nearly cooked through and browned.

3) Spread the cranberry sauce on pizza crust. Top it with brie, chicken; cover it with mozzarella cheese.

4) Bake it in oven for about 20 minutes.

21) Greek Style Spinach and Olives Pizza

"The bold flavour of Kalamata olives, spinach and Sun dried tomatoes makes this pizza tasty."

Prep Time: 30 minutes

Cooking Time: 12 minutes

Ready In: 42 minutes

Yields: 6 slices

Ingredients:

- ½ cup of mayonnaise
- 4 cloves of garlic, minced
- 1 (12-inch) Italian pizza-crust, pre-baked
- ½ small red-onion, thinly sliced
- ¼ cup of Kalamata olives, pitted and coarsely chopped
- 1 tsp of dry oregano
- ½ cup of sun-dried tomatoes (oil-packed), coarsely chopped
- 1 cup of feta cheese, crumbled and divided
- 1 tbsp. of oil from sun-dried tomatoes
- 2 cups of baby spinach-leaves

Directions:

1) Adjust the oven rack to low position; preheat the oven at 450 degrees. Combine garlic, mayonnaise and ½ cup of feta cheese in a bowl. Place the pizza crust over baking tray; spread the pizza with mayonnaise mixture and top it with olives, tomatoes, and oregano. Bake till crisp and heated through, for about 10 minutes.

2) Toss onion and spinach with 1tbsp of oil from sun-dried tomato. Top the pizza with the spinach mix and remaining ½ cup of feta cheese. Return the tray to oven; bake it till cheese melts, for about 2 more minutes. Cut the pizza into wedges and serve.

22) Cheesy Burger Pizza

"This pizza which tastes just similar to a burger is delicious with a special sauce, American cheese, and ground beef."

Prep Time: 25 minutes

Cooking Time: 20 minutes

Ready In: 45 minutes

Yields: 8 servings

Ingredients:

- ½ lb of ground beef
- 1 onion, chopped
- 1 (12-inch) pizza crust, pre-baked
- ½ tsp of seasoning salt
- 2 cups of lettuce, shredded
- 1 cup of American cheese, shredded
- 1 cup of thousand-island salad dressing
- Dill pickle slices (optional)
- 1 tomato, chopped (optional)

Directions:

1) Place onion and ground beef in skillet on medium-high heat. Cook and stir to crumble, till evenly browned. Season it with salt. Drain any excess grease, and keep aside.

2) Preheat oven at 450 F (230 C). Spread the salad dressing over pizza crust. Top it with onion and ground beef. Sprinkle with cheese over top.

3) Bake it in oven for about 8-10 minutes, till cheese melts. Allow it to cool for 5 minutes and slice it into wedges; Top it with pickles, lettuce and tomato, if desired.

23) Veggie Pizza with Ranch Dressing

"This pizza loaded with fresh vegetables is delicious. Any fresh vegetables can be used."

Prep Time: 15 minutes

Cooking Time: 15 minutes

Ready In: 30 minutes

Yields: 10 servings

Ingredients:

- 1 pizza crust, unbaked
- 1 lb of mozzarella cheese, shredded
- ½ cup of carrots, shredded
- ½ cup of cauliflower, chopped
- ½ cup of onion, chopped
- ½ cup of red bell-pepper, chopped
- 1½ cups of Ranch-style salad-dressing
- 2 cups of Cheddar cheese, shredded
- ½ cup of fresh broccoli, chopped
- ½ cup of fresh mushrooms, sliced

Directions:

1) Preheat the oven at 350 F (175 C).

2) Place the pizza crust over a baking sheet. Evenly spread the crust with dressing. Sprinkle it with the Cheddar cheese. Then layer it with cauliflower, carrots, broccoli, red pepper, onion, and mushrooms. Top it with shredded mozzarella cheese.

3) Bake it in oven for about 15-20 minutes, till vegetables become tender, and cheese melts and becomes lightly brown.

24) Cheesy Tuna Pizza

"This easy to prepare pizza is yummy and delicious to taste."

Prep Time: 10 minutes

Cooking Time: 20 minutes

Ready In: 30 minutes

Yields: 8 servings

Ingredients:

- 1 (8 oz.) pkg. of cream cheese, softened
- Crushed red pepper-flakes to taste
- ½ cup of red onion, thinly sliced
- 1½ cups of mozzarella cheese, shredded
- 1 (5 oz.) can of tuna, flaked and drained
- 1 (14 oz.) pkg. of pizza crust, pre-baked

Directions:

1) Preheat the oven at 400 F (200 C).

2) Spread softened cream-cheese over the crust. Sprinkle with onions and tuna on the pizza; top it with mozzarella cheese and red pepper-flakes.

3) Bake it in oven till cheese melts and begin to brown, for about 15-20 minutes.

25) Pepper and Onion Pizza

"The nutrient-packed ingredients used in this pizza make this a healthy recipe."

Prep Time: 10 minutes

Cooking Time: 12 minutes

Ready In: 22 minutes

Yields: 6 servings

Ingredients:

- 1 (12-inch) pizza crust
- 3 cups of bell peppers (red, yellow, green), chopped
- 3 cloves of garlic, crushed
- 2 tbsp. of extra-virgin olive-oil
- Salt, to taste (optional)
- Crushed red pepper-flakes, to taste (optional)
- ¾ cup of herbed feta-cheese, crumbled
- 1½ tsp of dry Italian herbs
- 1 cup of yellow or red onion, sliced and pulled into rounds

Directions:

1) Preheat the oven at 450. Place pizza crust over a baking sheet. Except cheese, combine the remaining ingredients in a mixing bowl; spoon the mixture over the crust.

2) Top it with cheese and bake in oven for about 10 to 12 minutes, or till vegetables become crispy-tender.

Thank you for reading my book. Your feedback is important to us. It would be greatly appreciated if you could please take a moment to REVIEW this book on Amazon so that we could make our next version better

Thanks!

Martha Stone

martha@168publishing.com

Printed in Great Britain
by Amazon